SCIENCE BEHIND THE COLORS
GOLDFINCHES

by Alicia Z. Klepeis

pogo

Ideas for Parents and Teachers

Pogo Books let children practice reading informational text while introducing them to nonfiction features such as headings, labels, sidebars, maps, and diagrams, as well as a table of contents, glossary, and index.

Carefully leveled text with a strong photo match offers early fluent readers the support they need to succeed.

Before Reading

- "Walk" through the book and point out the various nonfiction features. Ask the student what purpose each feature serves.
- Look at the glossary together. Read and discuss the words.

Read the Book

- Have the child read the book independently.
- Invite him or her to list questions that arise from reading.

After Reading

- Discuss the child's questions. Talk about how he or she might find answers to those questions.
- Prompt the child to think more. Ask: Did you know about goldfinches before reading this book? What more would you like to learn about them?

Pogo Books are published by Jump!
5357 Penn Avenue South
Minneapolis, MN 55419
www.jumplibrary.com

Copyright © 2022 Jump!
International copyright reserved in all countries.
No part of this book may be reproduced in any form without written permission from the publisher.

Library of Congress Cataloging-in-Publication Data

Names: Klepeis, Alicia, 1971- author.
Title: Goldfinches / by Alicia Z. Klepeis.
Description: Minneapolis, MN: Jump!, Inc., [2022]
Series: Science behind the colors | Includes index.
Audience: Ages 7-10
Identifiers: LCCN 2021033536 (print)
LCCN 2021033537 (ebook)
ISBN 9781636903767 (hardcover)
ISBN 9781636903774 (paperback)
ISBN 9781636903781 (ebook)
Subjects: LCSH: Goldfinches–Juvenile literature.
Classification: LCC QL696.P246 K54 2022 (print)
LCC QL696.P246 (ebook)
DDC 598.8/85–dc23
LC record available at https://lccn.loc.gov/2021033536
LC ebook record available at https://lccn.loc.gov/2021033537

Editor: Eliza Leahy
Designer: Emma Bersie

Photo Credits: Wildphotos/Shutterstock, cover; Mike Truchon/Shutterstock, 1; Janet Griffin-Scott/Alamy, 3; Glenn Bartley/BIA/Minden Pictures/SuperStock, 4; Daybreak Imagery/Alamy, 5; WilliamSherman/iStock, 6-7; FotoRequest/Shutterstock, 8, 17; rck_953/Shutterstock, 9; Gerald A. DeBoer/Shutterstock, 10-11; suefeldberg/iStock, 12-13t; MichaelStubblefield/iStock, 12-13b; Ivan Kuzmin/Alamy, 14-15; freebilly/iStock, 16, 18-19; Irh847/Getty, 20-21; Mark Hryciw/Dreamstime, 23.

Printed in the United States of America at Corporate Graphics in North Mankato, Minnesota.

TABLE OF CONTENTS

CHAPTER 1
Beautiful Birds................................4

CHAPTER 2
Fabulous Feathers..........................8

CHAPTER 3
Bright Beaks.................................16

ACTIVITIES & TOOLS
Try This!....................................22
Glossary....................................23
Index.......................................24
To Learn More..............................24

CHAPTER 1
BEAUTIFUL BIRDS

What bird is bright yellow in summer but brown in winter? It is an American goldfinch!

Goldfinches are **granivores**. This means they mainly eat seeds. **Flocks** of these beautiful birds often eat at bird feeders.

bird feeder

CHAPTER 1

Some goldfinches live on the edges of forests. Others live in plains or fields. In winter, their feathers are dull. This **camouflage** helps them blend in. They can hide from **predators** like snakes and weasels.

TAKE A LOOK!

Where do American goldfinches live? Take a look!

■ = where American goldfinches live

CHAPTER 1 7

CHAPTER 2
FABULOUS FEATHERS

How do goldfinches change colors? Like most birds, they **molt**. This happens twice a year. It takes up to eight weeks.

The spring molt happens before the **breeding season**. Males grow bright feathers to **attract** females. They turn brilliant yellow. This takes a lot of **energy**! They have black foreheads. Their wings are black and white.

male

female

CHAPTER 2 9

In fall, a male's feathers turn brown. Why? He doesn't need to attract a **mate** in winter. He sheds his bright feathers. This helps him save energy.

DID YOU KNOW?

Bright feathers stand out. This makes it easier for predators to see males. Dull colors help them hide.

CHAPTER 2

Like many birds, female goldfinches are dull all year. This helps protect them and their young.

In spring, they are olive on top. They have yellow feathers on their undersides. In fall, their feathers turn even more gray and brown.

Young goldfinches look dull, too. Their feathers are grayish brown. They grow brighter feathers less than a year after they hatch.

CHAPTER 2

CHAPTER 3
BRIGHT BEAKS

Goldfinches' beaks change color, too. Both male and female beaks turn bright orange in spring. Why? The birds eat fresh green plants, fruits, and flowers.

beak

These foods have **pigments**. Eating them makes the birds brighter. **Genes** affect color, too. In winter, it may be hard to find food with more pigments. This causes their beaks to turn gray.

CHAPTER 3   17

Females use their beak color to **communicate**. A female with a brighter beak is more **dominant**. Other females might avoid fighting with her. She may get the foods with more pigments.

> ### DID YOU KNOW?
>
> What if a bird is sick or **stressed**? Its beak color can fade. It can change in a matter of hours.

18   CHAPTER 3

CHAPTER 3

Goldfinches are known for their changing colors. Their bright beaks and fabulous feathers help them communicate and attract mates.

These birds are beautiful! Have you ever seen one?

DID YOU KNOW?

Beak and feather brightness show how healthy a bird is. Females are more attracted to brighter males.

ACTIVITIES & TOOLS

TRY THIS!

COLOR ON THE MOVE

Goldfinches' colors partly depend on what they eat. See how color moves through an object with this activity!

What You Need:
- measuring cup
- water
- glass jar or vase
- teaspoon
- red or blue food coloring
- spoon to stir with
- scissors
- ruler
- daffodil
- pencil
- notebook

1. Pour about 1 cup (237 milliliters) of water into the jar.
2. Add 3 teaspoons (15 mL) of food coloring to the water. Stir until mixed well.
3. Cut about 2 inches (5.1 centimeters) off the bottom of the daffodil stem.
4. Put the flower stem in the water. Leave it there overnight.
5. Check on the flower the next day. What happened to it? Record your results in your notebook.

GLOSSARY

attract: To get something's interest.

breeding season: The period of time when animals join together to produce young.

camouflage: A disguise or natural coloring that allows animals to hide by making them look like their surroundings.

communicate: To share information, ideas, or feelings with another.

dominant: Having power and influence over others in a habitat.

energy: The ability or strength to do things without getting tired.

flocks: Groups of birds of one kind that live, travel, or feed together.

genes: Parts of living things that are passed from parents to offspring and determine how one looks and grows.

granivores: Animals that mainly eat seeds.

mate: One of the breeding partners of a pair of animals.

molt: To shed feathers and replace them with new ones.

pigments: Substances that give color to something.

predators: Animals that hunt other animals for food.

stressed: Experiencing physical or mental tension.

ACTIVITIES & TOOLS

INDEX

beaks 16, 17, 18, 21
bright 4, 9, 10, 14, 16, 17, 18, 21
camouflage 6
communicate 18, 21
dull 6, 10, 13, 14
eat 5, 16, 17
fall 10, 13
feathers 6, 9, 10, 13, 14, 21
females 9, 13, 16, 18, 21
fields 6
fighting 18
flocks 5
foreheads 9
forests 6
hide 6, 10
males 9, 10, 16, 21
mate 10, 21
molt 8, 9
pigments 17, 18
predators 6, 10
seeds 5
spring 9, 13, 16
summer 4
wings 9
winter 4, 6, 10, 17
young 13, 14

TO LEARN MORE

Finding more information is as easy as 1, 2, 3.
❶ Go to www.factsurfer.com
❷ Enter "goldfinches" into the search box.
❸ Choose your book to see a list of websites.

24 ACTIVITIES & TOOLS